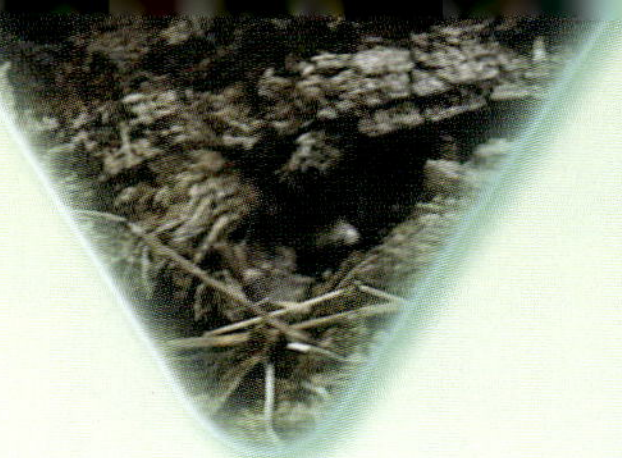

Otters at Home

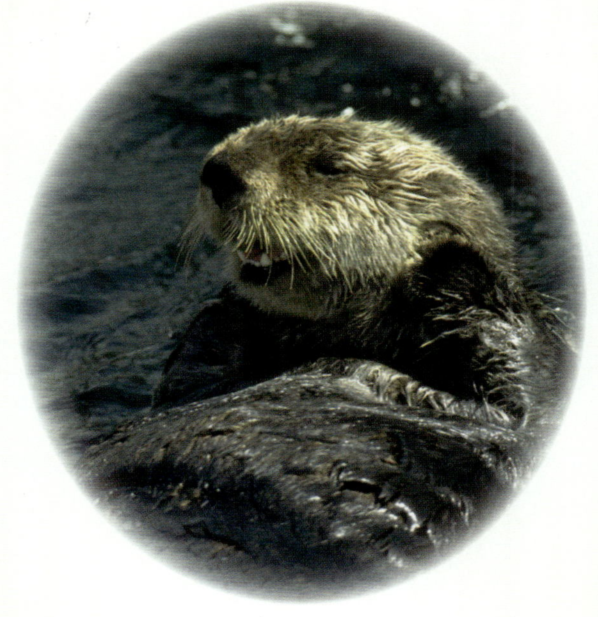

Alex Lane

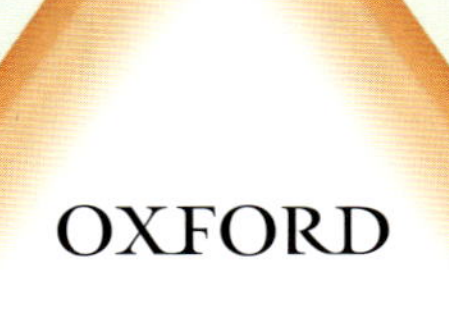

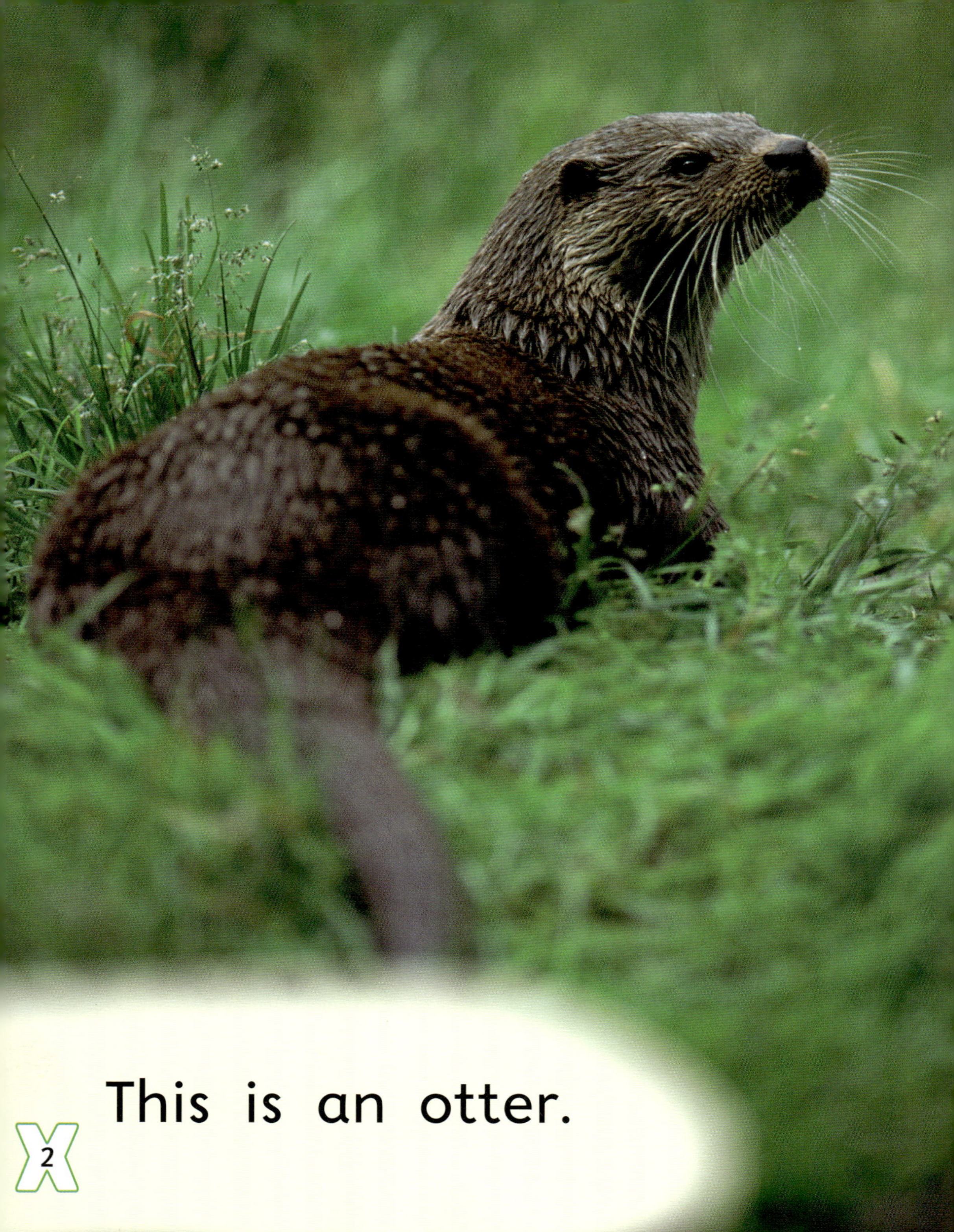

This is an otter.

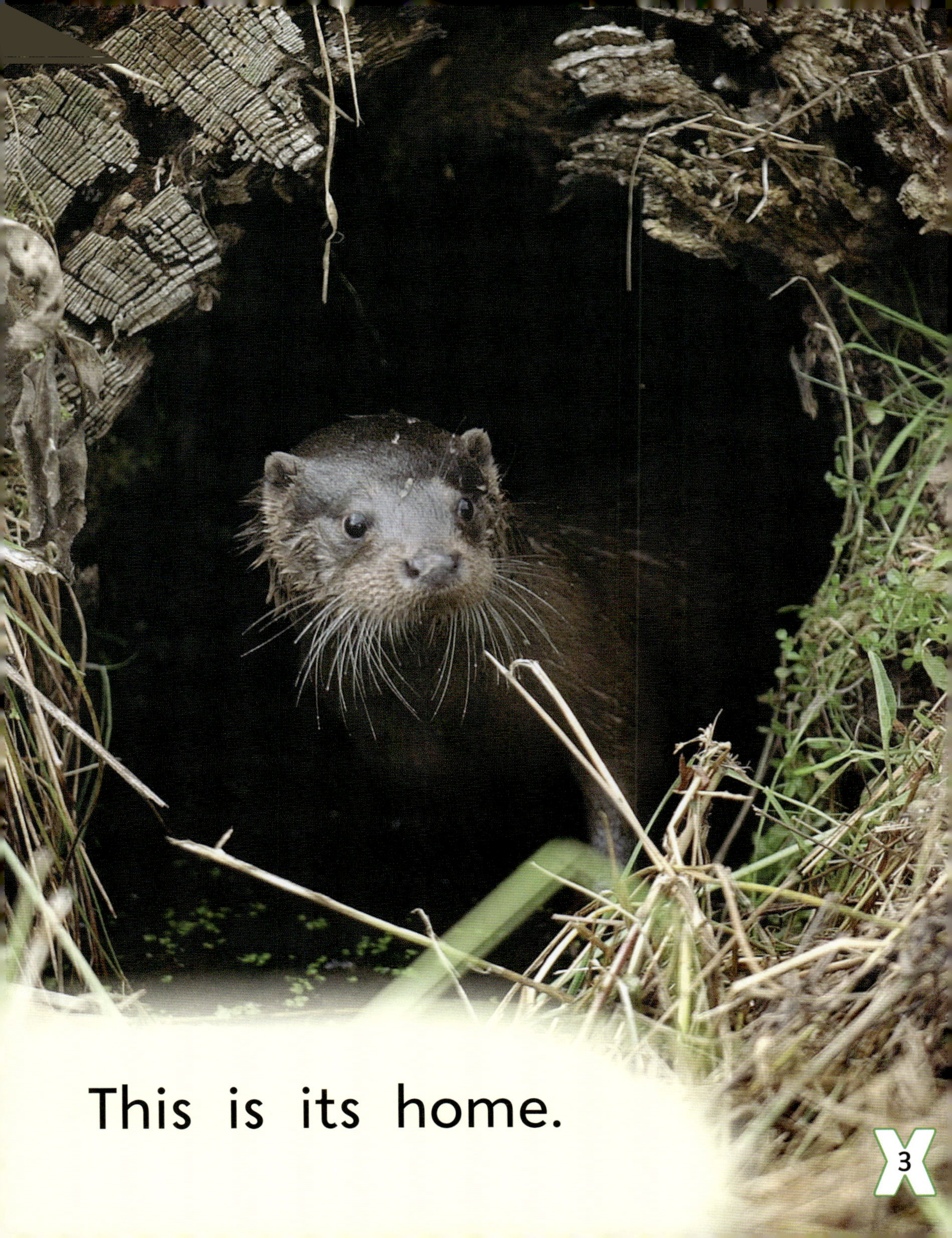

This is its home.

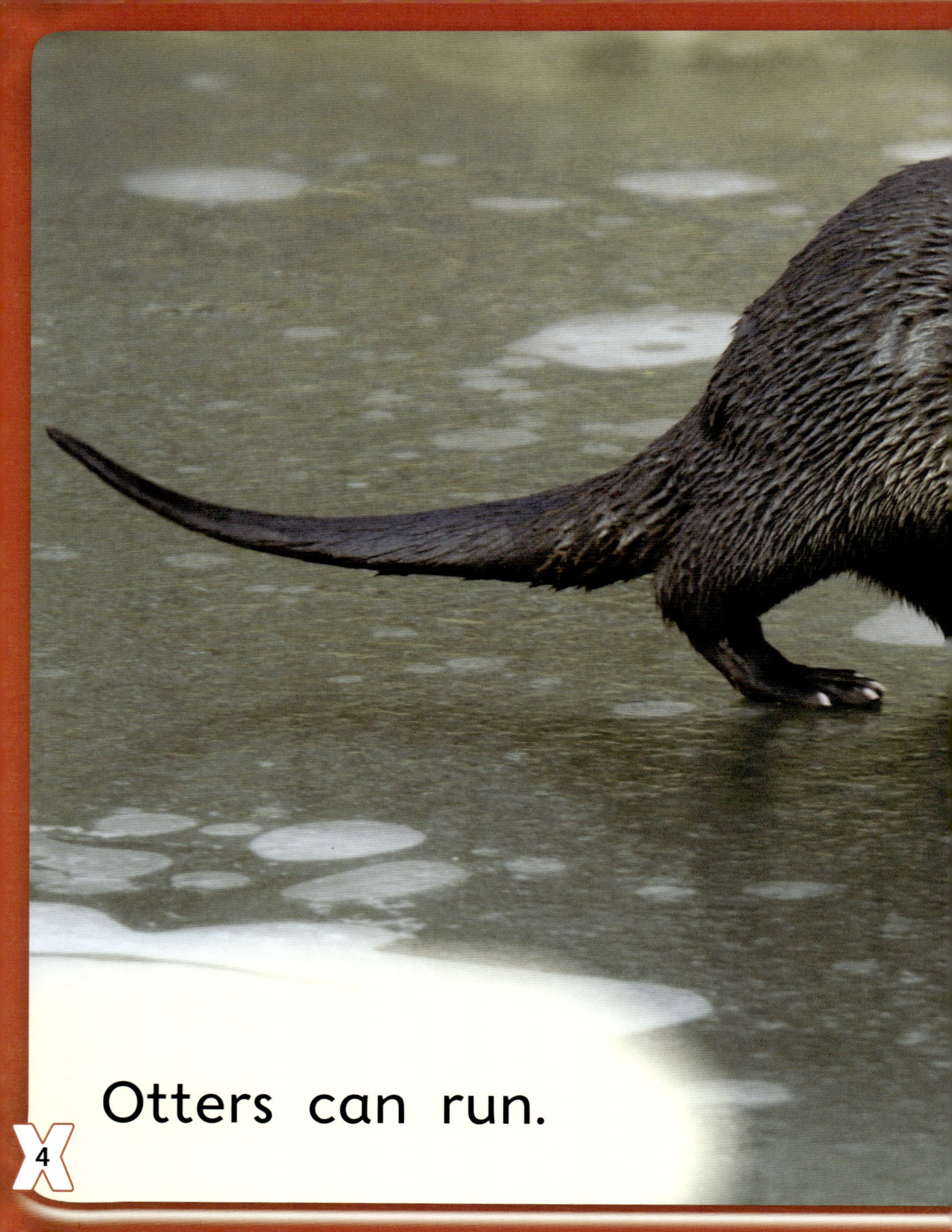

Otters can run.

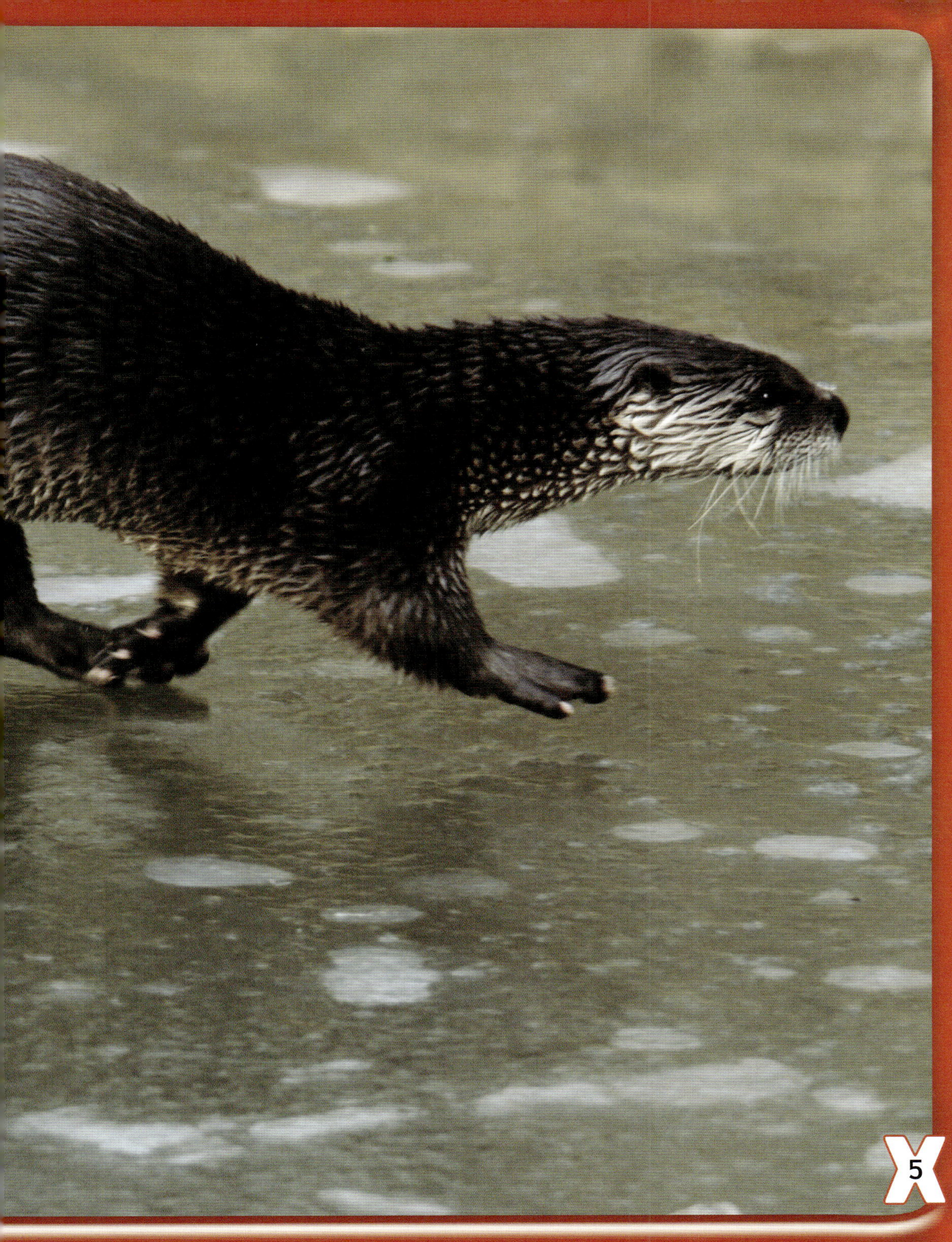

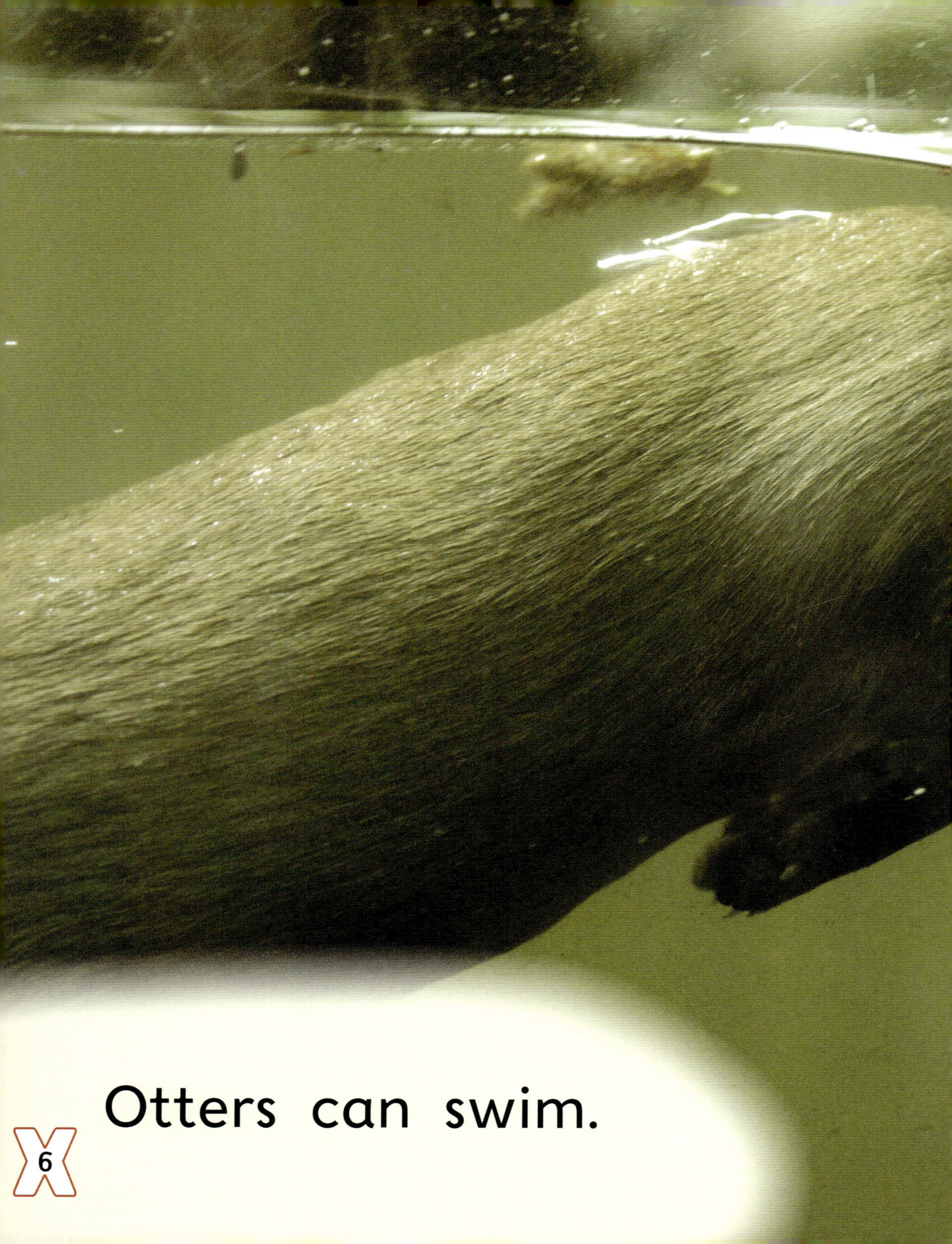

Otters can swim.

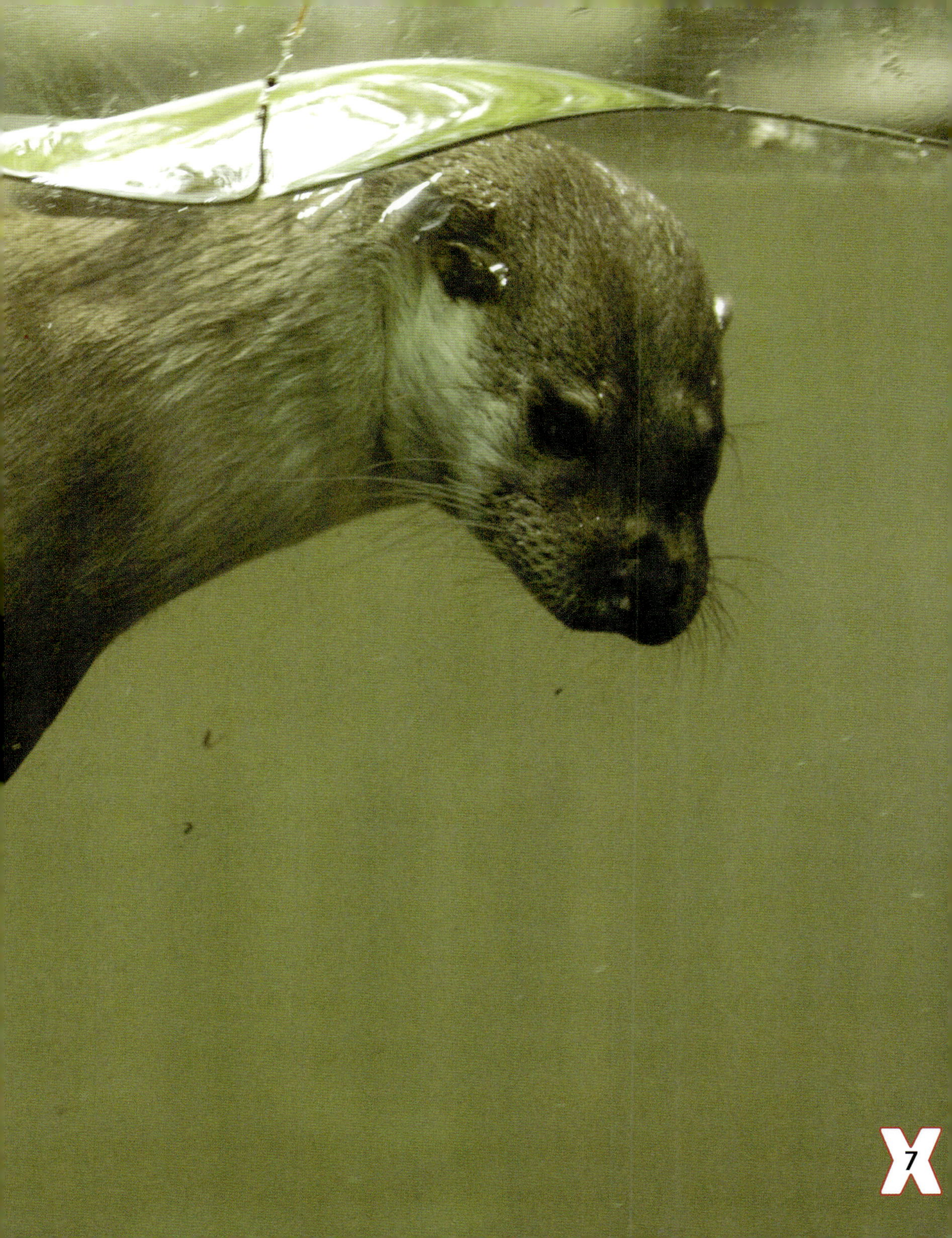

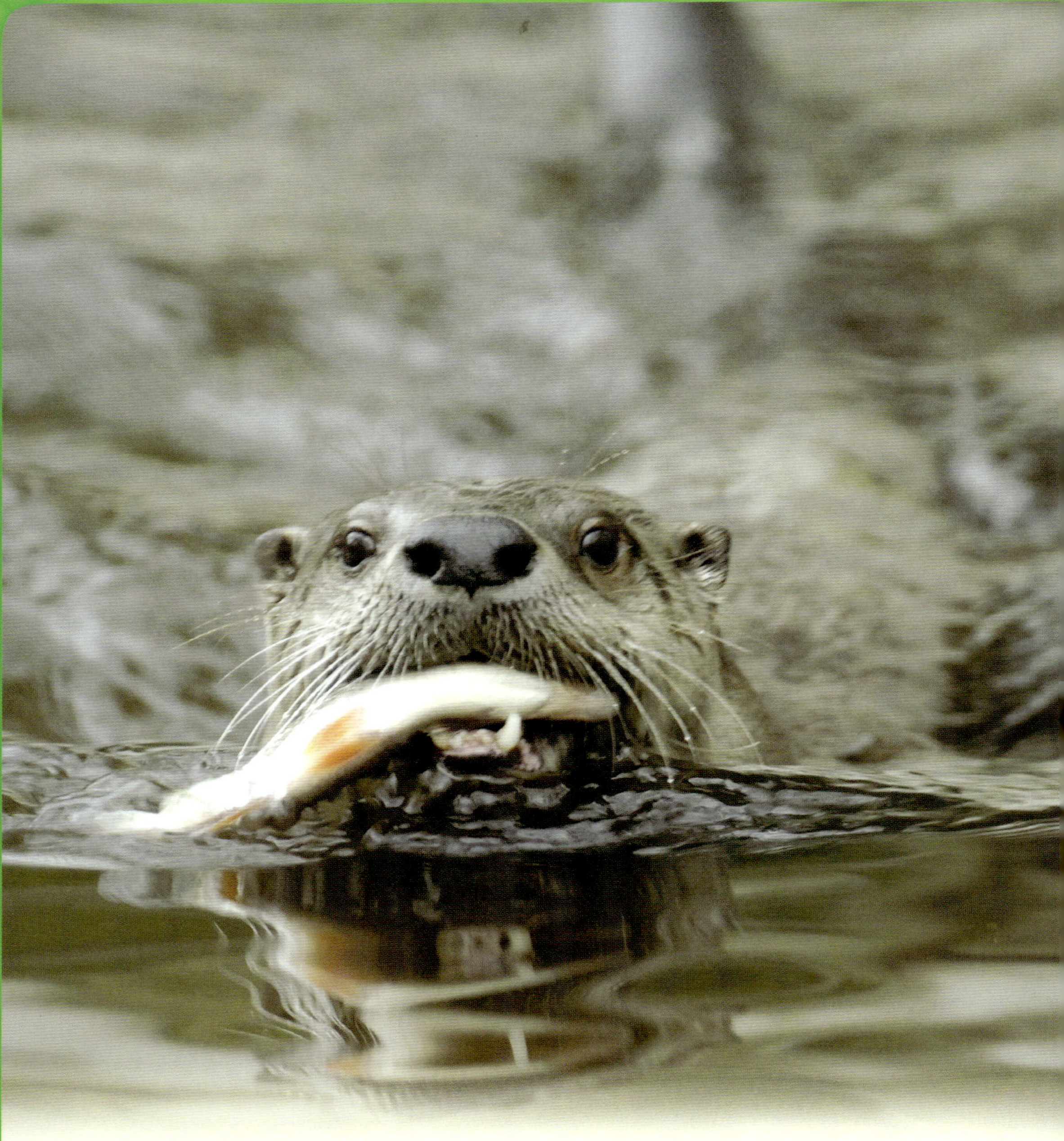

Otters can fish.

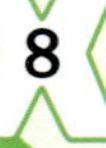

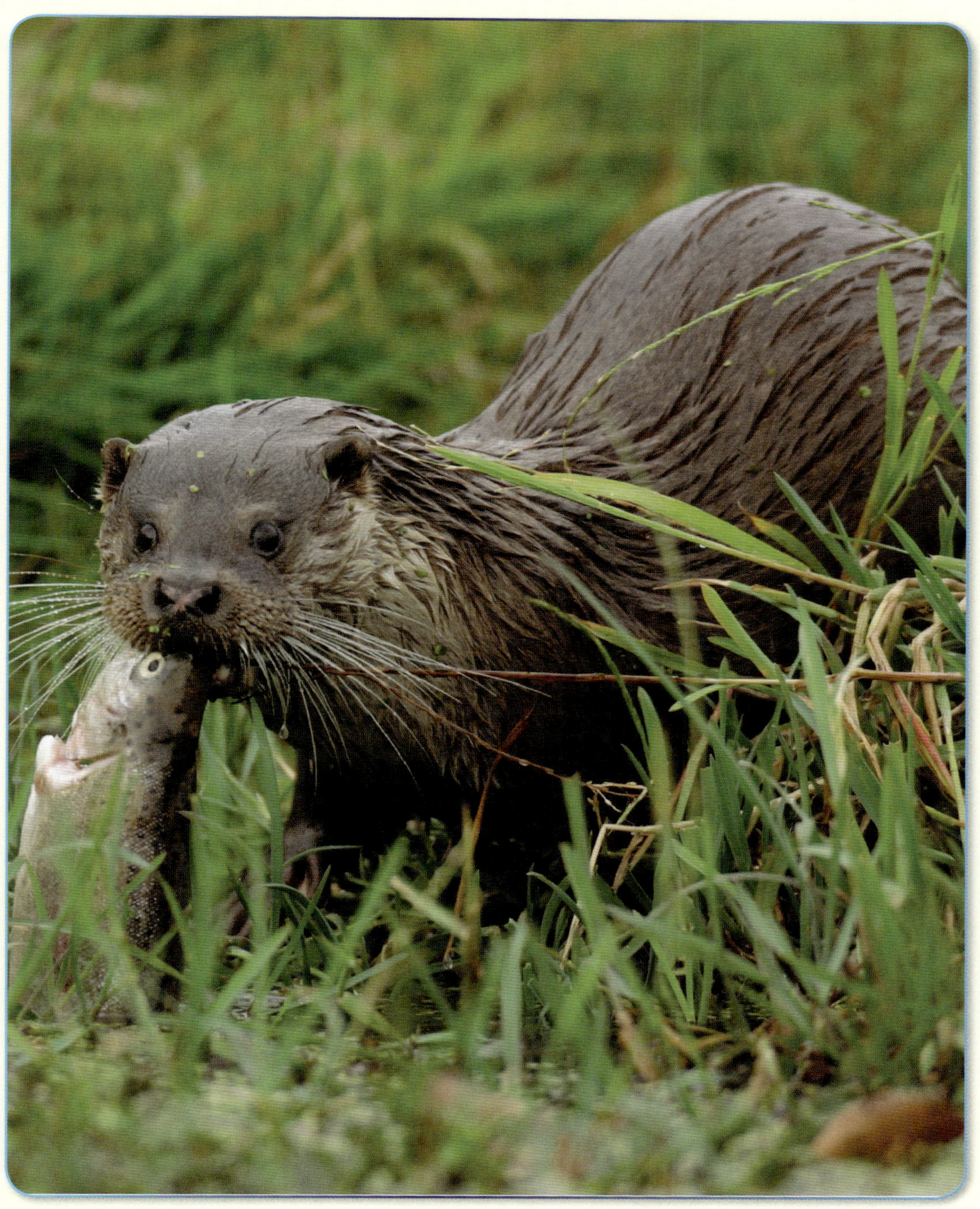

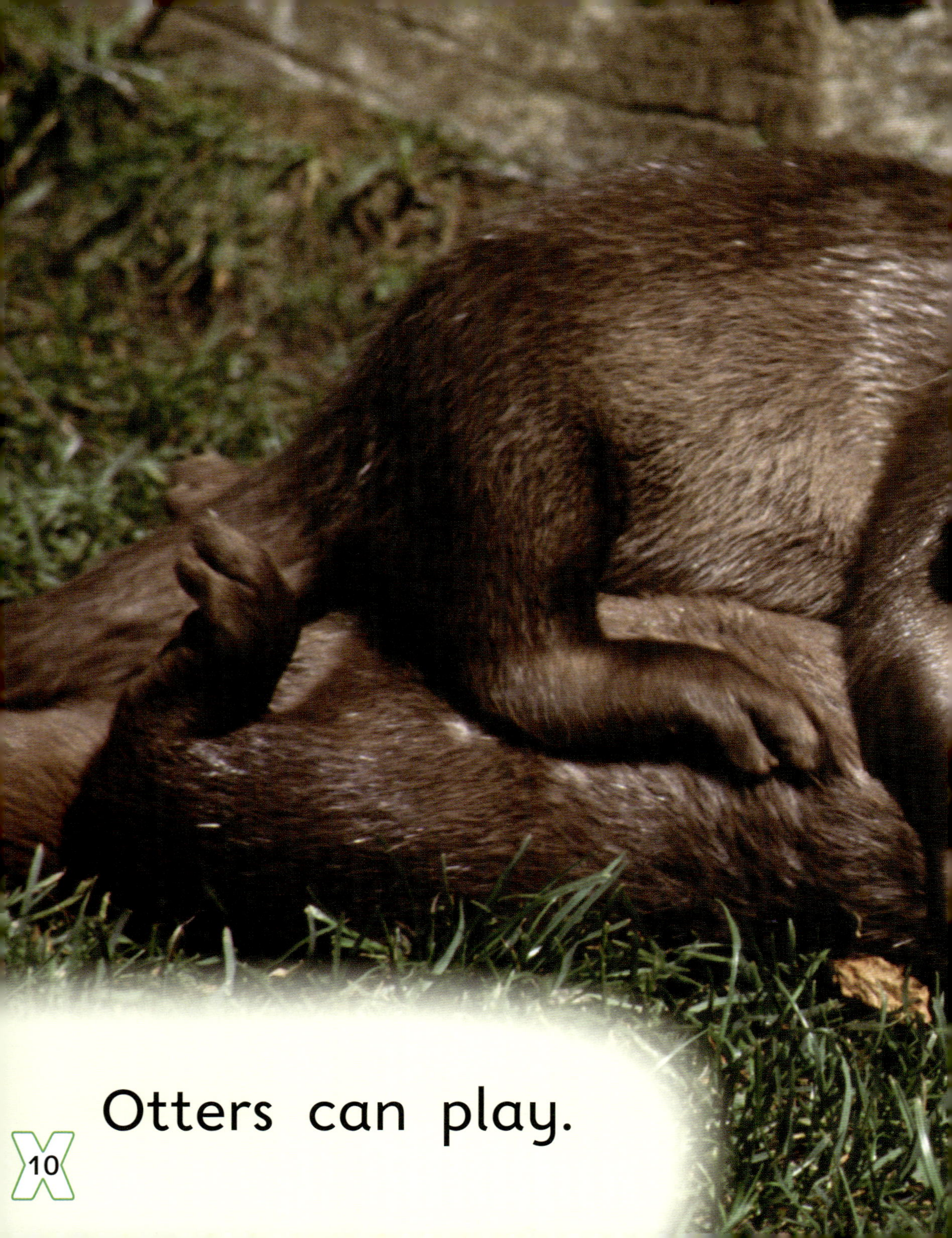

Otters can play.

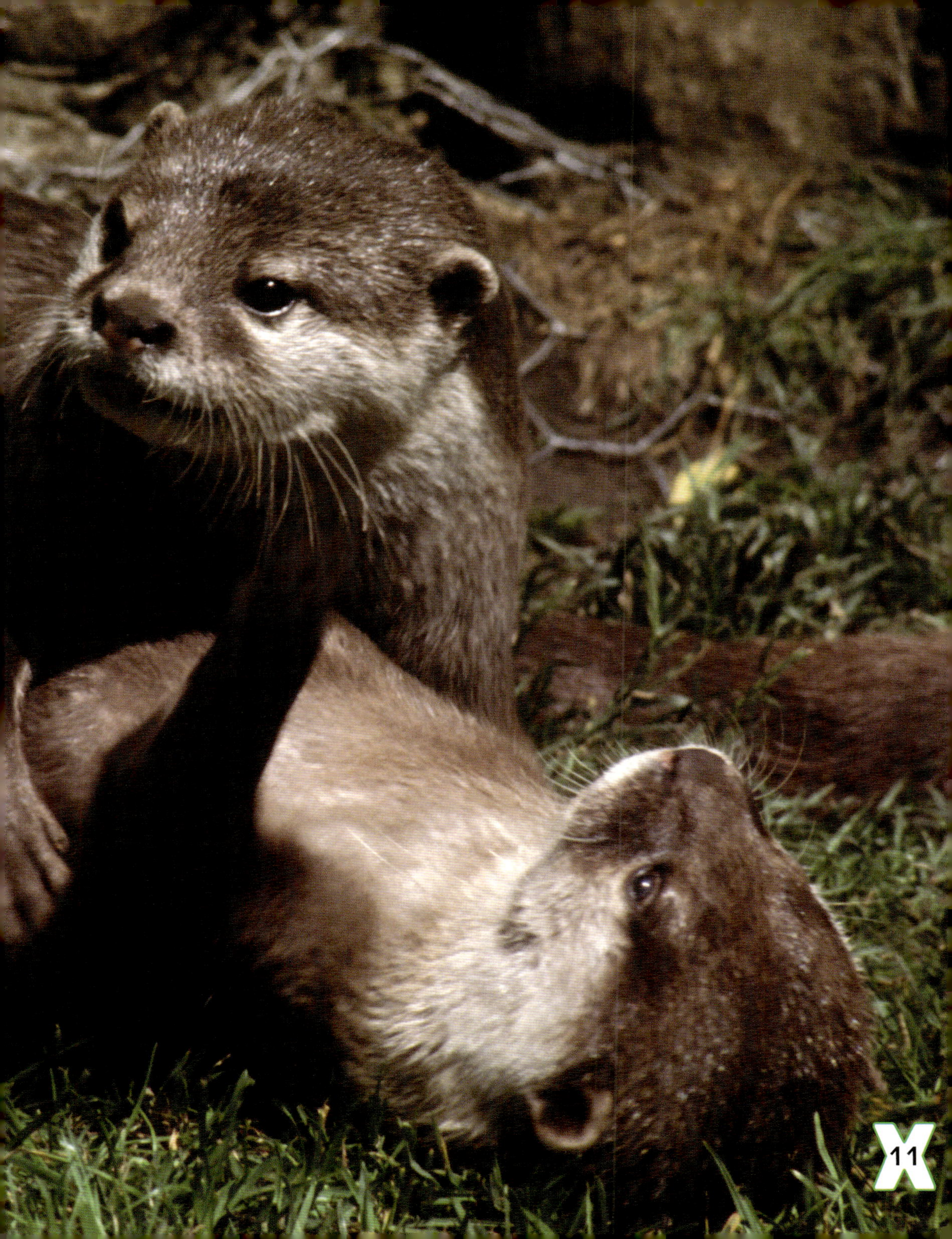

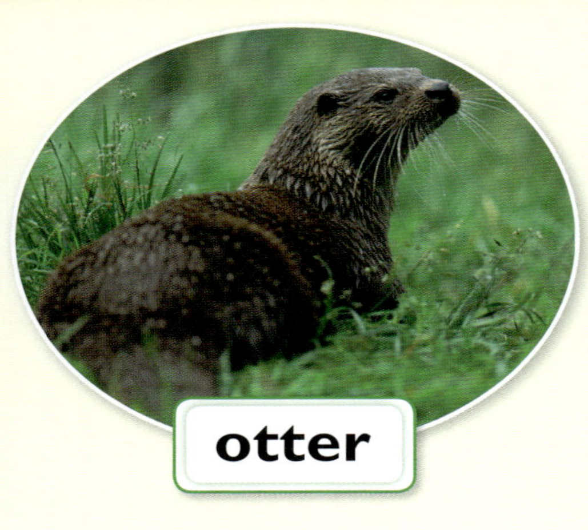

otter

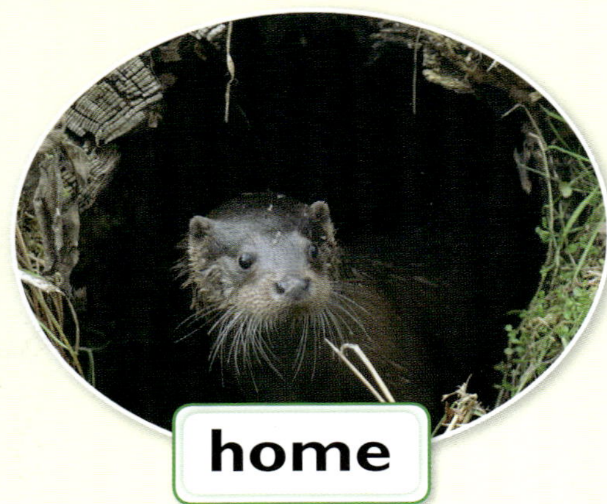

home

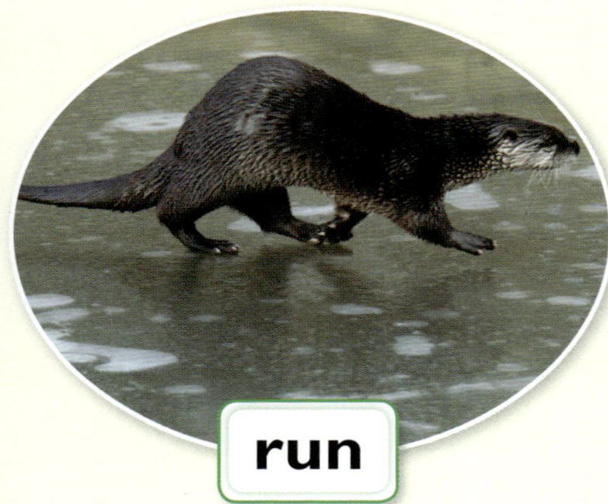

run

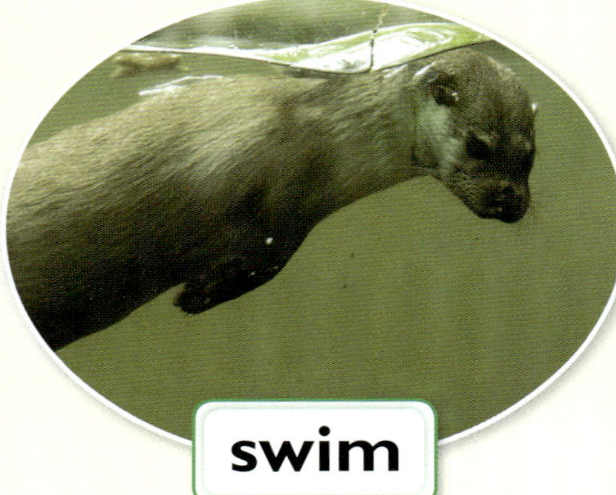

swim

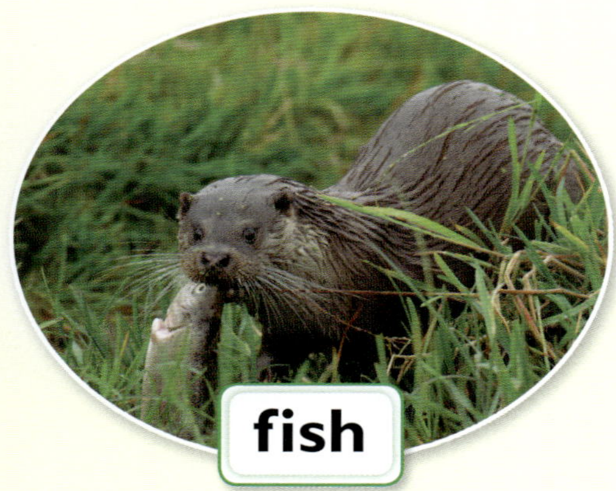

fish

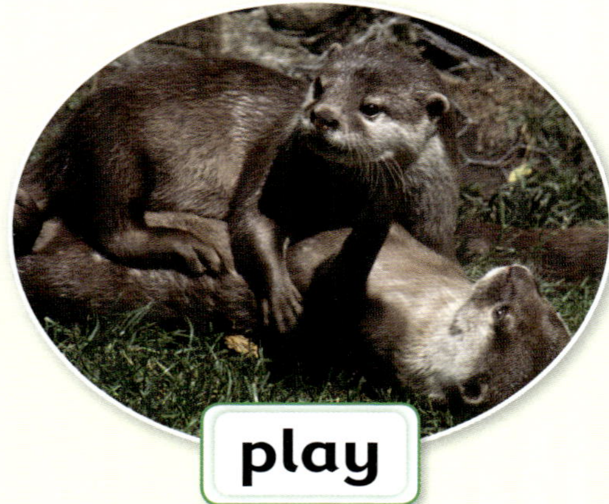

play